AWAKENING

THE GREAT FALLING AWAY

RICK BARNETT

NEWMAN SPRINGS PUBLISHING
320 Broad Street
Red Bank, NJ 07701

First originally published by Newman Springs Publishing 2022

ISBN 978-1-68498-439-8 (Paperback)
ISBN 978-1-68498-440-4 (Digital)

Printed in the United States of America

Introduction

This book is being written because I was compelled to write it. For months on end, my mind was consumed by things that Christians are doing wrong. It troubled me so much that I reached out to a pastor at church and poured out my heart, Pastor Dan, my beloved brother, teacher, and counselor who is one of many. Pastor Dan said, "Rick, it sounds like your heart is broken over what's going on, and I think you should tell the world about your broken heart."

Now I expect great criticism for what I'm about to write to you. But the criticism I will receive will be from those who are deceived. My honor for God and his ways are so much deeper now. Heaven is God's throne and the earth his footstool, and at his feet, we must serve. For if we do not serve the Kingdom of God, what good are we to heaven? This nation has lost its fear of God. My hope in this book will be to awaken the Christian soldier in all Christians, who are blinded and deceived by the world. I write this book for the Christians who are my beloved brothers and sisters in Christ, and I do this out of love, and love alone.

Awakening and Weeding the Spirit and not Seeing a Foreseeing of God's Provision

It was 2019, and I was at my mother's. It was Mother's day, and I had gone there to prepare a place for my mother to park her car so that she would not have to climb the stairs when she left to go to the store. My mother was ninety-one at the time. I was so afraid that she would fall when she left the house. I was so frustrated nothing seemed to be going as planned. I had so much trouble trying to level the ground where I was to lay the cross tying down to hold the gravel in place. It was getting to the point where I was getting angry because of all the delays.

Meanwhile, my mother wanted to prepare me fish for lunch. Isn't it funny how mothers always are looking for ways to serve us and try to make our lives better? I should have been taking her out and giving her a rest because it was Mother's Day. Little did I know something was going to happen. I was working at the back door, when I heard my mother scream out, "Oh no, oh no!" Then I looked up at the window by the door, and all I saw was a bright flash of light. I jumped to my feet and ran to the door. There my mother was lying on a blazing floor. I very quickly and gently pulled her to the next room. Then I grabbed a rug and smothered the floor out.

My wonderful mother did not want me to have cold fish with hot hush puppies, so she started a pan of oil on the eye, and guess what happened. She had tried to make her way to the back door with a flaming hot pan of oil spilling it as she walked barefoot to the back door. *Panic* set in. I ran to the refrigerator, grabbed a bucket of country crock, and proceeded to try to ease my mother's pain and torment. I was not waiting thirty minutes for an ambulance to come out into the county.

I could be at the hospital before then. So I placed her in the back seat, with flashers on, and horn blowing. We were off to the hospital, cursing all who slowed my progress on the way there. All the way there I was talking to the Lord. I did not know it at the time, but he was trying to tell me something, "Peace be still," but I would not realize it until the next morning. Finally, we made it to the hospital where she could get the help she needed. Only to find out that they could not help her. So she got her ambulance ride anyway.

There is no burn center in North Alabama. "Are you kidding me?" I said to the doctor frantically. Christ wasn't walking with me in this because I let the situation separate me from him. Again I would not realize this until the next morning.

The doctor said that they would send her to UAB in Birmingham. The doctor told me she had second-degree burns on her hands, her side, and her legs and feet. So I went to the house to pick up the things she wanted. On the way to Birmingham, I tried to talk to the Lord while driving to Birmingham, but the situation, traffic, and worrying about my mother were still blocking what he was trying to tell me all along. "Peace be still, Rick." Again I would not realize this until the next morning.

Finally I arrived at UAB, in the emergency room. The police officer inside the door told me that my mother's car would be okay where it was parked because the buses were not running that late in the day. So I went up and found my mother's room, gave her the things she requested, and made sure she was okay. I told my mother that I was going to get something to eat and fuel the car up. and I would be back. So I went downstairs to get the car, but when I got there the car was gone. It had been impounded by a street patrolman. It was 10:00 p.m. The officer at the desk gave me two phone numbers of cab companies to call. The cab companies I called had no cabs available for several hours, so I went back in and told the officer, and he said he was sorry. I went out into the hall, and once again looked up at the ceiling, and all I said was, "I could use a little help right now, Lord."

I started pacing back and forth wondering how I would get to my mother's car when all of a sudden, a female officer approached me and said, "Mr. Barnett, my supervisor said that I could take you to pay your fine and to take you to your car." So off we went to the police station to pay the fine. I went in and paid the fine. Finally I was on my way to pick up my mother's car, at the impound yard. I walked in with documents in my hand, only to find out that they would not release my mother's car to me because it was not in my name. They said they would need written confirmation from the owner, and I told her my mother cannot write because her hands are wrapped; she has been burnt. She said she would have to have verbal confirmation on hospital letterhead from the nurse on duty. So this officer drove me all the way back to the hospital.

On the way back I told the officer all that happened that day. She told me she understood, and that she also had a mother that she had to care for. We were at the hospital; it was now 11:00 pm. The officer said that she would wait for me and take me back to the impound yard. So I ran into the hospital and went to the nurses' station. I told the nurse what I needed, and she said that we would have to wake mother up. Then I lost control and shouted, "My mother's been through enough. You know that I am her son!" It became very silent you could hear a pin drop. It was now 11:30 p.m. We stood there looking into each other's eyes. Suddenly I was overwhelmed with guilt and shame. My eyes begin to fill with tears as I tried to tell her I was sorry and to forgive me, and that my day had been a train wreck all day long. She calmly said, "It's okay, I understand, but we have to follow protocol." We walked into my mother's room, and the nurse woke her up.

My mother woke up and saw me in the room, then she looked up at the clock on the wall, and ask me, "Son, what are you still doing here? You cannot sleep in this chair with your back problems. Please go home, and get some rest, and I'll see you tomorrow." It broke my heart to tell my mother the situation after the nurse had gotten all she needed to put down on paper. Then I was on my way again, back to the police station to obtain the document that would clear the impound yard of any responsibility.

At the police station, I quickly got the document I needed. The man behind the counter asked me if I had the keys. After the kind of attacks I had all day I thought it best to look in my pocket for the keys. "Yes," I replied here they are right here. It was now well after midnight. We rushed to the patrol car and off again to the impound yard. Finally at the impound yard, the officer gave me a card and told me, "Looks like you're on your way now. If there's anything I can do, please call me." And she said to be safe driving home. I told her that I didn't know what I would have done without her help that night.

Finally I walked into the office and had permission to go get my mother's car. A young man drove me back in a golf cart to my mother's car. I felt so relieved that I was finally going home to go to bed and get some rest and prepare myself for the next day. When I got out of the golf cart and ran my hand off into my pocket. Okay, *you* guessed it there were no keys. I quickly called the officer that had given me the card, and she said she would stop by the patrol station and go in, and see if anybody had turned in the keys, and if not check the perimeter and in the car for the keys.

Meanwhile I walked into the parking lot to see if they had fallen out as I had gotten out of the patrol car. It was now after 1:00 p.m. I walked inside the impound office and asked the lady at the desk if she had a phone charger I could borrow. My phone was almost dead. While waiting on my phone to charge, I sat there looking back at my day. I asked the Lord, "Why am I going through all of this?" Suddenly the phone rang it was the officer with more bad news; there were no keys to be found. I thank her again for all her time and effort.

The lady at the impound yard said she had a number of a locksmith that they used. I was ready to max out my credit card just to go home. So I called the number she gave me, after giving them the information about the car, make, and model, they told me the key had a chip in the key, and it would be 9:00 a.m. to 11:00 a.m. before a key could be made. I asked the lady at the desk if I could sleep in the backseat of my mother's car, and she told me that the insurance would not allow it! At ropes inn, I had to get out of there and find some quiet place to break down.

Looking at my phone before I walked out into the parking lot, I saw it was after 2:00 a.m. I started walking aimlessly around the parking lot. I finally work my way down to the main entrance of the parking lot. And there I fell on my knees hands lifted high, and I said, "Oh, Lord, my God, where are you?" I had to get up and move to the curb because there was a car coming. I watched and it looked as if a mother was bringing her son to get his car out of impound. Then I began pacing the parking lot once again. Then the lady in the office came out and said, "Mr. Barnett, you need to come inside." So I went inside. She said, "I may have good news for you." This lady found a set of keys as she was walking into the police station. I will dial the police station for you

When the officer answered I asked him about the keys that were found outside, then he asked me to describe the keys, so I did, then he told me, "Well, sir, looks like we have your keys." All I could say was, "Thank you, Jesus., I quickly called the officer that had helped me so much that night, and I asked her if she could bring me my mother's keys, and she said, "Sure, I will." I thanked the lady who had found my mother's key and began talking to her about my day. When the officer pulled up outside, I went out and got the keys, then I told her how much of a blessing she was to me that night and that morning, and then I gave her a big old hug.

Once again, I was in the golf cart, but this time I was going home. Just when I had gotten on Interstate 65, I breathed a sigh of relief. Then suddenly the Lord came to me. He began revealing things to my mind. He had made sure that I was working right beside the window in which I would see the flash of flame. He was there in the car to both rides to the hospitals, placing cars and tracks in my path to slow my pace for I couldn't see ahead. He was there when I needed transportation that night and help. He was there.

He was there when I was covered with shame and guilt asking for forgiveness from the nurse. He was there when I was pacing the parking lot and feeling lost and hopeless. Yes, and when I asked him where he was, he showed up bigger than life. All along he was in front of me. All along sweet Jesus was beside me, and behind me. And all along, he was trying to whisper in my ear, "Peace, be still. God and the Holy Spirit will put you in situations to awaken you—to awaken the Holy Spirit within you." We must not ever lose sight of Jesus, for if we do we struggle. Whatever I walk through now, I look back and remember all that he did for me through the ordeal, and all he wanted to do when I was not listening. So this is my testimony to my awakening!

In Matthew 5:13, Jesus teaches about a salty spirit: "You are the salt of the earth. But if the salt loses its saltiness, how can it be made salty again? It is no longer good for anything, except to be thrown out and trampled by men." It is my belief that Jesus is telling us if a seasoning has no flavor, it has no value. If Christians make no effort to affect the world around them, by the standards of the Kingdom of God, they are of little value to God. If we are too much like the world, we are worthless. Christians should not blend in with everyone else. We should make every decision we make with a Kingdom perspective! If we are to do God's will and bring heaven to earth as he desires, we must stand with him not against him. So always have a salty spirit, and be useful for the Kingdom of God. Now I feel I should go back to Deuteronomy and what Moses said, then still applies to us today.

> And now, O Israel, what does the Lord, your God, ask of you, but to fear the Lord your God, to walk in all his ways, to love him, to <u>serve</u> the Lord your God with all your heart, and with all your soul, and to observe the Lord's commands and <u>decrees</u> that I am giving you today for your own good! (Deuteronomy 10:12–13)

Often we ask, "What does God expect of me? Here Moses gives a summary that is simple in form and easy to remember. Here are the essentials: (1) Fear God (have reverence for him). (2) Walk in all his ways. (3) Love him. (4) Serve him with all your heart and soul.

(5) Observe his commands. How often do we complicate faith with man-made rules, regulations, and requirements? Are you frustrated and burned out from trying hard to please God? Concentrate on his real requirements and find peace, respect, follow, love, serve and obey!

God should always be the ultimate authority in a Christian's life! I am so glad that God sent me his son Jesus. I turn to him daily, but I always thank God daily. Because this is what he's always desired, for us to have reverence for him, to acknowledge him for all that he has given us. It's sad to say, but many Christians just go to church to hear a sermon that will make them feel better about what they did the previous week. And when they leave the church and get around the people outside the church, they generally fall back into the same old pit.

Many times in churches all over this nation, there is a lack of servanthood. Most pastors are always asking for help in one area or another. He does this because he is called to do this. But it is for you he is doing this, seeking out those with gifts, to not only help your brothers and sisters so that they may experience worship as you do every Sunday but to help you fulfill your obligation to God, to serve his house and to serve his son for the church is Christ's very body. Let me tell you from experience, serving Christ will give you deep roots in your faith and in what you believe. So awaken, Christian soldier, and serve because it is required of you. To awaken your spirit, awaken and serve, and you will feel what I am talking about.

> For even the son of man did not come to be served, but to serve and give his life as a ransom for many. (Mark 10:45)

Gay Marriage

Now it is time for the part in which the criticism that I spoke of at the beginning of the book. God's word is very specific, and it is not hard to understand. I have found no gray area in God's word or the gospels of Jesus Christ. In this section, I would like to clear up some things about what God says about our responsibility as Christians. The first topic I would Like to cover is gay marriage. Let's see what God's word says about this topic. Leviticus 18:22 said about this,

> Do not lie with a man as one lies with a woman: that is detestable. (Leviticus 18:22)

> Do not defile yourselves in any of these ways, because this is how the nations that I am going to drive out before you became defiled. Even the land was defiled, so I punished it for its sin, and the Land vomited out its inhabitants. But you must keep my decrees and my laws. The native-born and the aliens living among you must not do any of these detestable things. For all these things were done by the people who lived in the land before you, and the land became defiled. And if you defile the land, it will vomit you out as it vomited out the nations that were before you. Everyone who does any of these detestable things—such persons must be (cut off from their people). Keep my requirements and do not follow

any of the detestable customs that were practiced before you came and do not defile yourselves with them. I am the Lord your God! (Leviticus 18: 24–30)

Now to Romans 1:25–27,

Because of this, God gave them over to shameful lusts. Even their women exchanged natural relations for unnatural ones. In the same way, the men also abandoned natural relations with women and were inflamed with Lust for one another. Men committed indecent acts with other men and received themselves the due penalty for their perversion.

People tend to believe lies that reinforce their own selfish personal beliefs. Today more than ever, we need to be careful as Christians about the input we allow to form our beliefs. With TV, music, movies, and the rest of the media often presenting sinful lifestyles and unwholesome values, we find ourselves constantly bombarded by attitudes and beliefs that are totally opposed to the Bible. Be careful about what you allow to form your opinions. The Bible is the only standard of truth. Evaluate all other opinions in light of its teachings. Now just as Adam and Eve had great responsibility, so do we. God has given us as Christians the authority to place people in authority to rule this nation, and we are to place people there whose standards stand with God's morals. It is sad many who call themselves Christians do not stand with God, but for the world: Where do you stand? If you expect to enter heaven you must stand with God!

So awaken!

Gender

Now to cover the matter of gender

> So God created man in his own image, in the
> image of God, he created him (male and female),
> he created them. (Genesis 1:27)

How much more specific can God be than this. God made both man and woman in his image. Neither man nor woman is made more in the image of God than the other. From the beginning, the Bible places both man and woman at the pinnacle of God's creation. Neither sex is exalted, and neither is depreciated. Once again, God has given us as Christians the authority to place people in authority to rule this nation, and we are to place people there whose standards stand with God's morals.

Where do you stand in this matter with God or the world? Who are we to think that we know better what is good for God's creation, than he who created it? Why would you mock God? Do you not know how dangerous spiritually that is? Awaken, oh Christian soldier, and stand with God! For it is our choices here on Earth that we will be judged for. You must believe as a Christian, God does not make mistakes; we do!

Abortion

Now to cover the matter of abortion

Let's start out with the seventh commandment of God. "You shall not murder." If God lets a woman conceive, it is his wish that the child is born. Those who overrule God's decision are guilty of murder. Also, we must understand that those who give people the authority to let this be possible are also guilty of murder. We cannot wash our hands of our choices, because we will be judged for all of them.

In 2 Chronicles 28:3, Ahaz sacrificed his sons in the fire. Therefore the Lord his God handed him over to the King of Aram. He was also given into the hands of the King of Israel, who inflicted heavy casualties on him. Imagine the monstrous evil of a religion that offers young children sacrifices. God allowed the nation to be conquered in response to Ahaz's evil practices. Even today the practice hasn't abated. The sacrifice of children to the harsh gods of convenience, economy, and whim continues in sterile medical facilities in numbers that would astound the wicked Ahaz.

If we are to allow children to come to Christ, we must first allow them to come into the world. Do you not know that God has the answer to this; it's called a miscarriage. God is still the ultimate authority, always has been, and always will be. So make the right choice, and choose the Kingdom of God, and it will be well with your soul. Again we will all answer for our choices. Awaken and save your soul.

If you know anyone who is thinking about abortion, please read this Psalm over them.

> If I say, "Surely the darkness will hide me and the light become night around me," even the darkness will not be dark to you, the night will shine like the day, for darkness is as light to you.
>
> For you created my inmost being: you knit me together in my mother's womb. I praise you because I am fearfully and wonderfully made, your works are wonderful, I know that full well.
>
> My frame was not hidden from you when I was made in the secret place. When I was woven together in the depths of the earth, your eyes saw my unformed body. All the days ordained for me were written in your book. Before one of them came to be. (Psalm 139:11–16)

There is always answers guidance, love, hope, and healing in the Bible for those who seek it or need to hear it.

Lawlessness

Now for the matter of lawlessness

Read Ezekiel 5:3–7,

> But take a few strands of hair and tuck them away in the fold of your garment. Again take a few of these and throw them into the fire and burn them up. A fire will spread from there to the whole house of Israel.

This is what the Sovereign Lord says: This is Jerusalem, which I have set in the center of the nations, with countries all around her. Yet in her wickedness, she has rebelled against my laws and decrees more than the nations and countries around her. She has rejected my laws and has not followed my decrees.

Therefore this is what the Sovereign Lord says. You have been more unruly than the nations around you and have not followed my decrees or kept my Laws. You have not even conformed to the standards of the nations around you. From there it really starts getting bad. But for now, let's look at what this really means. 5:3–4 says "The few strands of hair Ezekiel put in his garment symbolized the small remnant of faithful people whom God would preserve. But even some from this remnant would be judged and destroyed because their faith was not genuine." Where will you stand in the coming judgment:

In Matthew, Jesus gives the sermon on the Mount. In 5:20, he tells us, "For I tell you that unless your righteousness surpasses that of the Pharisees and the teachers of the Law, you will certainly not enter the Kingdom of heaven." Jesus was saying that his listeners needed a different kind of righteousness altogether (love and obedience) not just a more intense version of the Pharisees' righteousness (legal compliance). Our righteousness must come from what God does in us, what we can do by ourselves is be God-centered, not self-centered. Once again he has given you authority to place people in authority, be based on reverence for God, not approval from people, and go beyond keeping the law to living by the principles behind the law.

Awaken, oh Christian soldier, and know that he is God, and do his will!

In Ezekiel, the people's wickedness was so great that they couldn't even keep the laws of the pagan nations around them, not to mention God's laws. Look at this nation. You see it every day, someone is always not submitting to authority. The laws are in place to protect the innocent. Not to give wicked people their own way. I admit some of the situations have gotten way out of hand, but so did the other person. It would be a lot simpler if they would just submit to the rule of law. We are turning into a lawless and godless nation. And the whole world will face judgment in the end.

In 2 Corinthians, Paul explained his concerns for the Corinthians' church:

> For I am afraid that when I come. I may not
> find you as I want you to be, and you may not
> find me as you want me to be. I fear that there
> may be quarreling, jealousy, outbursts of anger
> (<u>factions</u>), slander, gossip, arrogance, and dis-
> order. I am afraid that when I come again my
> God will humble me before you, and I will be
> grieved over many who have sinned earlier, and
> have not repented of the impurity sexual sin, and
> (<u>debauchery</u>) in which they have indulged.

The two words that I have marked in this section, I did not understand, so I sought knowledge of their meaning. Definition of *faction*—a group or clique within a larger group, party, government, organization, or the like. What about that, my brothers and sisters in Christ? Definition of *debauchery*—seduction from duty, allegiance, or virtue.

Do you see what I see in God's word? This tells me we have a moral obligation to God our creator. Awaken, awaken, awaken, and do what is right in the eyes of God.

Paul feared that the practices of wicked Corinth had invaded the congregation. He wrote sternly, hoping that they would straighten out their lives before he arrived. We must live differently than unbelievers, not letting secular society dictate how we are to treat others, or how we make our choices for the Kingdom of God, or in our nation.

Let us start at the beginning since the dawn of man and woman. They have been under attack by the evil one. He came to the garden to deceive Adam and Eve. You know the rest of the story, I hope. But we need to see that God knew that Satan was in the garden. He knew! But he allowed him in the garden to test the obedience of his creation. He is still testing us today! All God wants is for us to love him with all our hearts and all our mind, but to also fear him and his judgment. This is something that Christians in this nation have lost track of.

I was teaching a men's group, and the study was in Ezekiel. All Christians need to read this teaching of the nations that had lost the fear of God. Believe me when you read this, it will shake you to your very core. It will let you see how God hates immorality and spiritually, disconnection from him! God has given us all that we need. He has given us a roadmap to heaven which is his commandments and his decree and his word. He also gave us a moral compass which is Christ Jesus, not only a compass but a friend, healer, shepherd, counselor, redeemer, and general. We must follow him, or we lose our way and get off the path that we are to travel. As Christians, we must never lose sight of him.

To do that, we must feed the spirit for the spirit is much like the body; if it is not fed, it grows weak. We must do this daily, for a weak spirit is an easy prey for the evil one. So read your Bible daily, and be strong and courageous in the Lord for you have many battles to fight. God has given us heavenly armor so put it on, and fight the good fight. So awaken, oh Christian soldier, and stand and fight your battles, for you fight for the Kingdom of God. So awaken, oh Christian soldier, defender of the truth. So awaken, oh Christian soldier, believer and follower of Christ Jesus, our Lord and savior. So awaken, oh Christian soldier, for it is for your very own eternal life that you fight for.

Jesus tells us in Matthew 5:11:

> Do not think that I have come to abolish the
> Law or the Prophets: I have not come to abol-
> ish them but to fulfill them. I tell you the truth
> until heaven and earth disappear, not the small-
> est letter, not the least stroke of a pen, will by
> any means disappear from the Law until every-
> thing is accomplished. Anyone who breaks one
> of the least of these commandments. and teaches
> others to do the same will be called least in the
> Kingdom of heaven, but whoever practices and
> teaches these commands will be called great in
> the Kingdom of heaven. For I tell you that unless
> your righteousness surpasses that of the Pharisees
> and the teachers of the Law, you will certainly
> not enter the Kingdom of heaven.

Not everyone who says to me, "Lord, Lord," will
enter the Kingdom of heaven. (Matthew 7:21)

*Everyone really needs to listen to what Jesus is saying here,
"Awaken, but only he who does the will of my Father who is in
heaven.
　　*Jesus is very specific in what he says here.

Many will say to me on that day, "Lord, Lord, did
we not prophesy in your name, and in your name
drive out demons and perform many miracles?"
　　Then I will tell them (plainly), "I never knew
you, Away from me, you evildoers!" (Matthew
7:22–23)

*How would you like to get slapped in the face with that? When
we stand before our Lord and savior, as Christians, we should know
what God expects from us. He has made it very plain beginning in
Genesis to Malachi. About what is to become of us if we do not live
for him, and his ways. God's not looking for excuses he's Looking
for obedience. He has even sent us Jesus to guide us, so there are
no excuses. You must understand and awaken your mind. That in
the final judgment Christians will be judged just as severely as those
who are lost and do not know him. Why is that, you say! Because
as Christians we should know better. I could not help myself but
write this book because it has consumed my mind! Some will tell me
that this is not God's word. But this is what I see in God's word and
believe it to be true. Awaken and save yourselves, those who stand
against God and his wishes. Build your house on the rock that is
Christ Jesus. Awaken and do the will of God. Because doing his will
is not too much to ask, for someone who offers so much!

Now all has been heard; here is the conclusion
of the matter; Fear God and keep his commandments, for this is the whole duty of man.

For God will bring every deed into judgment, including every hidden thing, whether it is
good or evil. (Ecclesiastes 12:13–14)

In his conclusion, Solomon presents his antidotes for the two
main ailments presented in this book. Those who lack purpose and
direction in life should fear God and keep his commandments. Those
who think life is unfair should remember that God will review every
person's life to determine how he or she has responded to him, and
he will bring every deed into judgment. Have you committed your
life to God, both present and future? Does your life measure up to
his standards?

Your duty as a child of God is to obey him. You are to obey his
commandments and his decrees. In God's eyes, there is no excuse
for not doing this! Because if you do not stand with God, you stand
against him plain and simple. In the entire Bible, it speaks of only
good or evil. That is why every decision you make with the authority
God has given, you must line up with his Kingdom! If we cannot
line up with his Kingdom, what good are we to his Kingdom? As
Christians, we are soldiers of the one true God. Why else would he
give us spiritual armor? Our duty as Christians is to try our best to
bring heaven to Earth! How in the name of God can we do this if we
stand against him? This position of the world called parties or politics
is nothing more than good or evil.

God granted us free will so that we could choose our own fate!

The Bible speaks of the marks of God or Satan. I tell you
the truth it is we who choose which mark we bear. Now I ask you
Christian which mark do you bear. I want to reflect on Jesus's teachings on this matter:

Not everyone who says to me, "Lord, Lord,"
will enter the Kingdom of heaven, but only he
who does the will of my Father who is in heaven,

Many will say to me on that day, "Lord, Lord, did we not prophesy in your name, and in your name drive out demons and perform many miracles?" Then I will tell them plainly, "I never knew you. Away from me, you evildoers!" (Matthew 7:21–23)

Remember what Jesus said:

Do not think that I have come to abolish the Law or the Prophets, I have not come to abolish them but to fulfill them. I tell you the truth until heaven and earth disappear, not the smallest Letter, not the Least stroke of a pen, will by any means disappear from the law until everything is accomplished. (Matthew 5:17–18)

Anyone who breaks one of the least of these commandments, and teaches others to do the same will be called least in the Kingdom of heaven, but whoever practices and teaches these commands will be called great in the Kingdom of heaven. For I tell you that unless your righteousness surpasses that of the Pharisees and the teachers of the Law, you will certainly not enter the Kingdom of heaven. (Matthew 5: 19–20)

When governments fear, follow, serve, and obey the Lord, "it will be well" (1 Samuel 12:14). When governments disobey and rebel against God's good plans, "the hand of the Lord will be against you and your King.

"Being religious" (going to church, serving on a committee, giving to charity) is not enough if we do not act out devotion and obedience to God.

What is being obedient to God to obey his commandments and his standards for Life. Is it God's standard that a man should lie with another man or a woman to another? No, and as a Christian, you know this. Does anyone have the right to say that they are a woman when they are a man? No, and as a Christian, you know this too! And does God allow life that he has put into a worm to be put to death? Again no, and as a Christian, you know this also!

So why then do you stand against God?

James submit yourselves to God

What causes fights and quarrels among you? Don't they come from your desires that battle within you? You want something but don't get it. You kill and covet, but you cannot have what you want. You quarrel and fight. You do not have it because you do not ask God. When you ask, you do not receive because you ask with wrong motives, that you may spend what you get on your pleasures,

You adulterous people. Don't you know that friendship with the world is hatred toward God? Anyone who chooses to be a friend of the world becomes an enemy of God. Or do you think Scripture says without reason that the spirit he caused to live in us envies intensely? But he gives us more grace. That is why Scripture says:

> God opposes the proud but gives grace to the humble. Submit yourselves then to God. Resist the devil. And he will flee from you. Come near to God, and he will come near to you. Wash your hands, you sinners, and purify your hearts.

You double-minded.

How can you come near to God? If you do not yield to his authority and will, commit your life to him and his control and be willing to follow him. Don't allow Satan to entice and tempt you. When you know God's standards, make your choices for this nation by his standards.

Wash your hands and purify your hearts and lead a pure life for God!

Be cleansed from sin, replacing your desire to sin with your desire to experience God's purity. Repent and humble yourself before the Lord with your choices for this nation, and he will lift you up! Humbling ourselves means recognizing that our worth comes from God alone. To be humble involves working with his power according to his guidance, not with our own independent effort. Although we do not deserve God's favor, he reaches out to us in love and gives us worth and dignity, despite our human shortcomings.

But to put it very plainly. When you make your choices involving *his* creation and *his* moral standards, you are either for the world or for the Kingdom of God!

If you stand with those who oppose God's standards and give them the power to overturn God's standards, then you are just as guilty of defying and mocking God.

> Jesus says plainly, "If you defy God, you will never see heaven. If you call yourself a Christian, you must awaken, and wash your hands and submit yourselves before God. (Matthew 7:21–23)

Take a look at the word of God:

> He said, "If you listen carefully to the voice of the
> Lord your God and do what is right in his eyes,
> if you pay attention to his commands and keep
> all his decrees, I will not bring on you any of the
> diseases. I brought on the Egyptians, for I am the
> Lord, who heals you." (Exodus 15:26)

> Appoint judges and officials for each of the tribes
> in every town the Lord your God is giving you,
> and they shall judge the people fairly.
> Do not pervert justice or show partiality,
> Do not accept a bribe for a bribe blinds the eyes
> of the wise and twists the words of the righteous,
> Follow justice and justice alone, so that you may
> live and possess the land the Lord your God is
> giving you. (Deuteronomy 16:18–20)

That is just by God's law, not man's! These verses anticipated a great problem the Israelites would face when they arrived in the promised land. Although they had Joshua as their national leader, they failed to complete the task and choose other spiritual leaders who would lead the tribes, districts, and cities with justice and God's wisdom. Because they did not appoint wise judges and faithful administrators, rebellion and injustice plagued their communities. It is a serious responsibility to appoint or elect wise and just officials. In your sphere of influence—home, church, school, job—are you ensuring that justice and godliness prevail? Failing to choose leaders who uphold justice can lead to much trouble as Israel would discover. So it is also with our nation.

There is evil working within Christ's body which is in many churches.

Do not love the world or anything in the world.
If anyone loves the world, the love of the Father
is not in him.

For everything in the world—the cravings
of sinful man, the lust of his eyes and the boast-
ing of what he has and does—comes not from
the Father but from the world. The world and its
desires pass away, but the man who does the will
of God lives forever. (1 John 2:15–27)

When our attachment to possessions is strong, it's hard to
believe that what we want will one day pass away. It may be even
harder to believe that the person who does the will of God will live
forever. But this was John's conviction based on the facts of Jesus' life,
death, resurrection, and promises. Knowing that this evil world and
our desires for its pleasures will end can give us the courage to control
our greedy, self-indulgent behavior and to continue doing God's will.

The Bible is full of warning, after warning, after warning. Here
are just a few examples in the bible. You must read Ezekiel, for this
is where our nation is today. Ezekiel saw a vision that revealed God's
absolute moral perfection. God was spiritually and morally superior
to members of Israel's corrupt and compromising society. Ezekiel
wrote to let the people know that God was also present in Babylon
not just in Jerusalem. Today we are Babylon!

Because God is morally perfect, he can help us live above our
tendency to compromise with this world. Where we focus on his
greatness, he gives us the power to overcome sin and to reflect on his
holiness. We cannot excuse ourselves from our responsibilities before
God! We are accountable to God for our choices. Rather than neglect
him, we must recognize sin for what it is—rebellion against God—
and choose to follow him instead. All our choices must line up some-
how with the Kingdom of God. If we cannot do this as Christians
what good are we to the Kingdom of God! Ezekiel condemned the
Shepherds (unfaithful priests and leaders) who led the people astray.

Satan has divided the churches in our nation! Yes, you heard me
right. He has divided us into those who stand with the world and

those who stand with the Kingdom. For too long, our leaders in this nation have drawn Christians astray, by taking their eyes off of the Kingdom and focusing on the world. Sadly Jesus says that they have no chance to enter the Kingdom of God. Read Matthew 7:21–23 for yourself. If you cannot stand with God, you stand against him. And there in itself, you yourself have chosen the mark you choose to bear! Repent, oh Christians, and come back to the open arms of the Kingdom of God.

As a Christian, you know that the disobedience in heaven was cast out long ago! What makes you think he would let that environment back into his Kingdom! I beg of you to repent because you are nothing more than wolves in sheep's clothing within my Lord's body, a hypocrite of God's word and the teaching of Jesus Christ, and yes a disease within my Lord's body. Again please repent and regain your inheritance in the Kingdom of heaven.

How much more do you need to see in God's word to convince you of the sin you are committing against God! Can you not see with your own eyes that this nation has turned into Babylon? Can you not see in this nation and around the world that God is pouring the wrath out of his hand over the Earth! How much more will God break your heart to convince you to repent. Let me tell you God has provided enough followers in Christ's body, to overturn the ruling of this nation. Can you not see the faction in my Lord's body?

In 2 Corinthians, Paul explained his concerns for factions in the church; it's all in the bible, and it's all happening right now! How much more can I plead with those who say they know Christ. Because Christ himself tells them that he does not know them! In Matthew 7:23, I'll tell you again to read your bible. Your salvation depends on your knowledge, and it's on you to seek this knowledge! So wash your hands, you sinners, and purify your hearts, you double-minded, and submit yourselves to God. All of our shepherds, our priests, our pastors, and teachers. It is the responsibility of these people to lead them back to God!

Christ's body is divided by faction. These people I speak of should call this out for what it is disobedience to God's Laws, his decrees, and his moral standards. If you are afraid, you will lose people in your congregation because you called them out. It is their pride that drove them away not you or the truth of God's word, but their disobedience to God and his word. As a church we must stand as one with God, with no division about what he commands, no faction to intervene with our decision to do right in God's eyes.

Remember teachers the letters to the churches in revelation.

I do not know what more to say. So at this point, I will leave you with your thoughts and the word of God.

Yours sincerely,
Just a watchman
P. S.

I urge you to start reading the 119th Psalm 1–176. This will help you stay on the right path in your journey to the Kingdom. I urge you to read your Bible, for it is the only truth there is! This is both the longest psalm and the longest chapter in the Bible. It may have been written by Ezra after the temple was rebuilt as a repetitive meditation on the beauty of God's word and how it helps us stay pure and grow in faith. Psalm 119 has twenty-two carefully constructed sections, each corresponding to a different letter in the Hebrew alphabet and each verse beginning with the letter of its section. Almost every verse mentions God's word. Such repetition was common in the Hebrew culture. People did not have personal copies of the Scriptures to read as we do, so God's people memorized his Word and passed it along orally. The structure of this psalm allowed for easy memorization. Remember, God's word, the Bible, is the only sure guide for living a pure life!

We are drowning in a sea of impurity. Everywhere we look we find a temptation to lead impure lives. How do we stay pure in a filthy environment? We cannot do this on our own but must have counsel and strength more dynamic than the tempting influences around us. Where can we find that strength and wisdom? By reading God's word and doing what it says. Hiding or keeping God's word in our hearts is a deterrent to sin. This alone should inspire us to memorize the scriptures. But memorization alone will not keep us from sin; we must also put God's word to work in our lives, making it a vital guide for everything we do!

Most of us get irritated under the rules. for we think they restrict us from doing what we want. But God's laws were given to free us to be all he wants us to be. They restrict us from doing what might cripple and keep us from being our best. God's guidelines help us follow his path and avoid paths that lead to destruction.

The psalmist says that he is a *stranger on earth*, and so he needed guidance. Almost any long trip requires a map or guide. As we travel through life, the Bible should be our road map, pointing out safe routes, obstacles to avoid, and our final destination. We must recognize ourselves as pilgrims, travelers here on earth who need to study God's map to learn the way. If we ignore the map, we will wander aimlessly through life and risk missing our real destination.

Our lives are cluttered with rule books, but the authors never come with us to help us follow the rules. But God does! That is the uniqueness of our Bible. God not only provides the rules and guidelines but comes with us personally each day to strengthen us so that we can live according to those rules. All we must do is invite him and respond to his direction. Contrary to what we often expect, obeying God's laws does not inhibit or restrain us. Instead, it frees us to be what God designed us to be by living God's way. We have the freedom to fulfill God's plan for our lives.

To walk safely in the woods at night, we need a light so we don't trip over tree roots or fall into holes; in this life we walk through a dark land of evil. But the Bible can be our light to show us the way ahead so we won't stumble as we walk through this life. It reveals the roots of false values and philosophies.

Study the Bible so you will be able to see your way clear enough to stay on the right path. Double-minded people cannot make up their minds between good and evil. But when it comes to obeying God, there is no middle ground. You must take a stand! Either you are obeying him or you are not. Either you are doing what he wants or you are undecided. Choose to obey God, and say with confidence that you love his laws. The Bible is like medicine for the spirit. It goes to work only when we apply it to the affected areas. As you read the

Bible, be alert for lessons, commands, and examples that you can put into practice. Now put my book down and read the true book now, it is for your own good.

Love,
Rick

CPSIA information can be obtained
at www.ICGtesting.com
Printed in the USA
BVHW091853111122
651747BV00002B/463